GLITTER, GRIT & GROWING UP

A JOURNEY THROUGH GIRLHOOD, A STRAWBERRY LIPSTICK STATE OF MIND AND THE PATH TO FIND YOUR FORCE

KEIRA MUNIM

Contents

PART I

”So will you do it or not?”

”What” I hadn't heard what she had said.

I was too focused on my dinner.

“The marathon?”

A marathon?! Me?!

“uh sure what catagories are there”

“4K ,10K, half and a full”

Oh my god these are the options?!

“The 4K sound okay”

A 4k run seemed manageable; I'd done short races before, and while it wasn't my favourite activity, I knew I could handle it. But then, reality hit when I saw the registration forms.
Keira Munim - registered for a 10K marathon on-WAIT WHAT?

I wasn't signed up for a 4k—it was a 10k marathon. A sense of panic washed over me as I tried to search for the help centre

"Mom, are you sure this is right?" I asked tilting the screen towards her with disbelief. "This says 10 kilometers."

She looked up from the kitchen counter and smiled, her usual calmness radiating. "It's fine. If you can't finish, you can always walk. What matters is that you show up, try your best, and finish what you can. "Her words were comforting, but they didn't stop the nerves from creeping in. I had never run a distance like this before. What if I couldn't finish? What if I embarrassed myself? Oh god what if I pass out in the middle of the track and some poor medical volunteer has to carry me back. The thought of quitting halfway made me uneasy, but somehow, knowing my mom didn't expect me to be perfect helped ease some of that fear. Maybe it really was just about showing up.

It was five thirty in the morning. Cold and windy , not something I ever got used to in this Mumbai type of climate. The horn for the runners to assemble blared , and my nerves were at an all-time high. The sky was still dark and no sign of a sunrise yet. My legs felt stiff, and I couldn't tell if it was the early hour or the anticipation. Either way, I knew today was going to be tough.

My brother was indifferent, as usual, treating it like just another casual run. He always had this laid-back attitude about everything, which only made my anxiety worse. He used to train to run so this whole this was just going to be just another run for him .To make it worse he wasn't even doing the 10K ,he was doing the 4K. I tried to remember my mother's words "Just show up, try your best, and it'll be fine". There were hundreds of people at the line , all lacing up their shoes, warming up, and chatting excitedly. The smell of fresh grass and the energy in the air made it all seem so much bigger than I had imagined. My heart raced, and I felt a knot in my stomach and my heart in my throat.

"How are you feeling?" my mom asked, giving me an encouraging smile from the other side of the track.

"Great," I lied.

I glancing at the other runners. Some looked like they'd been doing this for years. Their athletic gear and confident strides made me feel out of place, but then I remembered: I was here, I had shown up, and that already felt like a small victory. As we waited for the start, I focused on calming my thoughts. I thought about how far I had come just by being there. My mom's words echoed in my mind, and I started to feel a strange sense of calm amidst the chaos around me. I wasn't expected to win. I wasn't even expected to finish. But I was expected to try. Standing at the starting line, I took a deep breath, feeling the cool air fill my lungs. Around me, the crowd of runners seemed to stretch endlessly. Everyone was buzzing with excitement, chatting, and stretching. Meanwhile, I stood still, trying to ground myself in the moment. The doubts crept back in. What if I couldn't even make it halfway? What if my legs gave out after just a few kilometers? My mother, looking completely at ease, gave me a thumbs-up. "You've got this," she said casually, as if it were the most obvious thing in the world. But I wasn't so sure. As the announcer's voice came over the speakers, signaling the start of the race, a wave of anxiety rushed through me. My heart pounded in sync with the growing excitement of the crowd. I looked around at the seasoned runners, feeling out of place. But then I reminded myself: showing up was half the battle.

As the countdown began, I took another deep breath. I wasn't here to be the fastest or the best. I was here because I believed I could try. And that belief, no matter how small, was enough to push me forward. When the race started, I moved, one foot in front of the other, fueled by that simple belief. The first few kilometers weren't so bad. My legs found a rhythm and my harry styles playlist really was the only thing keeping me going then. As I ran, I tried to focus on the sights—the tall trees lining the roads, and the sound of feet pounding the pavement around me. I noticed the occasional runner giving me a nod of encouragement, and it helped. But then, around the 5-kilometer mark, the fatigue started to set in. My legs felt heavier with each step, and my breath became shallow. The initial excitement had worn off, replaced by a deep exhaustion.

I started to question whether I could actually finish. Just as I was about to slow down, I heard someone behind me shout, "Chalo chalo! You're almost there!" It wasn't directed at me specifically, but in that moment, it felt personal. I glanced at the runner beside me, who seemed just as tired but determined. It was as if their strength rubbed off on me, and I pushed forward, reminding myself that I had come this far. Stopping now wasn't an option. The mental battle became just as intense as the physical one. My mind kept telling me to stop, to slow down, to take it easy. But somewhere, beneath the fatigue, a voice reminded me why I was there. I had shown up. I had committed to trying. And now, I just had to keep believing. As the race entered its final kilometers, my legs felt like lead, and every breath was a struggle. I could feel the sweat dripping down my face, my heart pounding in my chest. But there, in the distance, I could see the finish line. The sight of it gave me a burst of energy I didn't know I had. My body was tired, but my mind was focused. I had come too far to quit now. Step by step, I edged closer, the cheers of the crowd growing louder with each stride. The closer I got, the more real the moment became. The sun began to rise. The streets were lined with cheering spectators, holding signs and calling out encouragements. The energy of the race was infectious, and for a while, I forgot about my earlier doubts. With each step, the pain in my legs seemed to disappear, replaced by a surge of adrenaline. I could see my mom in the crowd, waving, cheering me on. It was enough to push me through those final moments. I saw my brother ,this is where our two tracks had aligned near towards the ending. The finishing line in sight and my brother by my side ,I crossed the finish line, a wave of relief and joy washed over me. I had done it. I saw my father cheering for me and recording me on his phone I had finished the 10k, and I had done it in under two hours.

Crossing that finish line wasn't just about completing the race; it felt like I had unlocked something within myself that I didn't even know existed. Each step toward the finish line was a testament to my resilience, not just physically but mentally. My body had been pushed to its limits, but the real battle was waged in my mind. Every muscle ached, my lungs burned, and yet, I kept moving. With every step, I was breaking through barriers of doubt, fear, and uncertainty. I realized that the race was more than just a test of endurance—it was a journey of self-discovery.

Before this marathon, I had always thought that physical challenges were about strength and stamina. But now, standing at the finish line, gasping for breath and drenched in sweat, I knew it was about something far deeper: the will to continue when everything in you screams to stop. The will to keep pushing forward when the easiest option is to quit. That day, I learned that my legs didn't carry me across the finish line—my mind did. The sense of accomplishment I felt was overwhelming. I had started the day unsure of myself, unsure if I could even run 10 kilometers. But as I crossed that line, the doubts that had clouded my mind for so long seemed to vanish. I had faced my fears head-on, and I hadn't let them stop me. That feeling—that rush of pride and exhilaration—was unlike anything I had ever experienced before. It was as if, in that moment, I had proven to myself that I was capable of so much more than I had ever imagined.

The lesson I learned was simple, yet profoundly life-changing. Showing up is half the battle. In life, in challenges, in everything we do, the mere act of stepping up, of being present, is a victory in itself. So often, we talk ourselves out of things before we even begin. We let fear of failure, of embarrassment, of not being good enough stop us from even trying. But by showing up to that marathon, I had already won half the battle. I was there, standing at the start line, ready to give it my best shot. That in itself was an accomplishment. But I realized something even more crucial—showing up is not enough. The other half of the battle, the half that truly counts, is believing in yourself. I could have easily given up halfway through the race. I could have let my doubts consume me, telling myself that I wasn't fit enough, fast enough, or strong enough. But I didn't. Somewhere along the course, amidst the struggle and the sweat, I found the strength to believe in my ability to finish. And that belief, that inner conviction, carried me through to the end. Finishing the marathon wasn't just about checking off a box or proving something to others. It was about proving something to myself. It was about recognizing that the biggest limitations in my life weren't physical or external—they were mental. The fears and doubts that had held me back were self-imposed. And by finishing the race, I had broken through those limitations.

This realization gave me a newfound sense of confidence, one that extended far beyond the race itself. It wasn't just about running anymore; it was about how I approached life. Every challenge, every obstacle, every dream that seemed too big or too distant no longer felt insurmountable. I had shown myself that I had the strength to persevere, and more importantly, the belief that I could succeed. That marathon was a turning point. It taught me that life is full of moments where we stand at the start line, unsure of what lies ahead. We have two choices: we can back down, letting fear dictate our actions, or we can show up and believe that we are capable of achieving more than we think. And when we choose to believe in ourselves, when we choose to take that leap of faith, we unlock a potential within us that is far greater than we ever imagined. In the end, it wasn't the medal or the time on the clock that mattered—it was the lesson I took away. Life, much like that marathon, will always present challenges that seem impossible at first glance. But I now know that by simply showing up and believing in my ability to overcome those challenges, I can accomplish things I once thought impossible. That day, I crossed more than just a finish line. I crossed into a new understanding of what it means to truly believe in yourself.

PART II

Here I am, at the cusp of one of the biggest changes of my life. University is on the horizon, and while I haven't even applied yet, it looms large in my thoughts every day. It feels like this huge, inevitable next step that everyone keeps talking about, but one that I haven't quite grasped myself. There's this pressure building—like a timer ticking down—and I'm caught somewhere between fear and anticipation. The fear comes in waves. Sometimes, I wonder, *How on earth am I going to improve my grades enough to get into the university I want?* Will my best be good enough? Will I be able to handle the academics, or will I struggle to keep up? Self-doubt creeps in when I least expect it. But then there's this spark of excitement too—the thrill of what's to come, of stepping into a new life where everything is fresh and full of possibilities. Yet, with all the excitement comes an undeniable pressure.

This won't just be a small step; it's a giant leap. The stakes feel higher than ever, knowing this shift is going to shape so much of my future. Am I ready for it? Do I have what it takes to succeed? These questions echo in my mind, and though I don't have all the answers yet, one thing is clear: this is going to be a big change, whether I'm prepared or not. As much as I try to focus on the excitement, the fear of the unknown is always there, lurking. It's the kind of fear that makes you question everything—every decision, every step forward. The idea of leaving home is terrifying in itself. Home has always been my safe space, the one place where I know I can retreat when things get tough. University feels like a whole new world, and once I leave, will I still have that safety net? What if I get homesick? What if I don't fit in? The thought of making new friends adds another layer of anxiety. I've spent years building friendships, and the idea of starting over is daunting. Will I find people I connect with? Will I have to change who I am to fit in? The fear of being alone in a sea of new faces is real, and sometimes, I wonder if I'm ready to take that on. And then, there's the academic pressure. University is going to be a different level of intensity. I've heard countless stories about how the workload is overwhelming, and I can't help but wonder if I'm ready for that challenge.

What if I can't keep up? What if my grades suffer? These thoughts often spiral into a deeper fear—what if I'm not cut out for university at all? What if I've been underestimating how hard it will be? Despite these fears, there's also this sense of inevitability. University is the next chapter, whether I like it or not. It's a stage of life that I can't avoid, and that in itself is scary. I'm scared of the unknown, scared of failing, scared of being unprepared. And yet, even with all this fear swirling around, I know deep down that this is something I have to face. It's the next step on the path I'm meant to take, and no matter how scared I am, I can't stay in one place forever. But alongside the fear, there's this quiet, unwavering belief that everything will work out. Somehow, amidst the anxiety, I know I'll get into university. I know I'll find my way. There's this deep-rooted confidence that no matter what, I'll succeed, and more importantly, I'll find happiness in this new stage of life. I don't know how it will happen yet, but I trust that it will. I often catch myself daydreaming about what life will be like once I'm there. I can picture it so clearly—walking through a bustling campus, meeting new people, diving into subjects I'm passionate about.

There's excitement in the idea of living in a new city, of growing both personally and academically. I see myself thriving, embracing the opportunities that come my way, and feeling a sense of accomplishment for making it to this new chapter. In those moments, the fear fades a little. I remind myself that I've faced change before and come out stronger. I remember the times I've succeeded in things I once thought impossible. And though the future feels uncertain, there's a part of me that knows I'll be okay. I'll find my footing, I'll make friends, I'll adjust to the academic challenges. The opportunities awaiting me outweigh the fears, and that brings me a sense of calm amidst the chaos of uncertainty.

Still, it's not easy. The internal battle rages on—one part of me clings to the familiar comforts of home, while the other is eager for the adventure that lies ahead. Some days, I feel ready for the change, excited even, while other days, the fear feels overwhelming, like a weight on my chest. I find myself talking to friends and family about it, seeking reassurance. Everyone says the same thing: "You'll be fine. You'll love it there." And while I appreciate their support, the fear is something only I can confront. No amount of reassurance can fully quiet the nerves that come with such a big life transition. But despite the fear, I know I'll adapt. I always have. It's in these moments of doubt that I remind myself that change, no matter how daunting, is something I can't avoid. It's a part of life, and resisting it only makes it harder. So, I tell myself that it's okay to feel scared, it's okay to be unsure. Change doesn't come with a roadmap, and there's no perfect way to navigate it. But I've faced challenges before, and this is just another one I'll learn to handle. There comes a point when fear starts to lose its grip. Gradually, I begin to accept that this shift to university, as scary as it feels, is inevitable. And more than that, it's necessary. I look back on past moments where I was scared of change—moving schools, starting new jobs, meeting new people—and I realize that every single one of those experiences led to growth.

With that in mind, I start to embrace the idea of the unknown. I let go of the need to control every detail and instead trust that things will work out the way they're meant to. I remind myself that change is a constant in life, and while it may bring uncertainty, it also brings new opportunities. There's a strange comfort in accepting that I can't predict everything, and that's okay. This shift in mindset brings with it a sense of peace. I'm still scared, yes, but I'm also excited. I'm ready to face the unknown, to step into this next chapter with an open heart, knowing that it's through these experiences that I'll continue to grow and evolve. And so, I come to the realization that change, as terrifying as it may seem, is part of life's natural progression. It's the catalyst for growth, for learning, for becoming a better version of yourself.

The fear of the unknown will always be there, but it doesn't have to hold you back. In fact, it's through embracing that fear that you find the strength to move forward. Change is inevitable, and that's okay. It's okay to feel scared, to feel uncertain, but it's also okay to trust that you'll find your way. And as I prepare for this shift to university, I'm learning to accept that while I may not know what lies ahead, I do know one thing for sure: I'll face it with courage, and I'll come out stronger on the other side.

PART III

Shifting to a new school was harder than I expected. It wasn't just about adjusting to a new environment—it was the struggle to make friends, keep up with academic expectations, and find my place amidst a sea of unfamiliar faces. From the start, I was putting in effort. A lot of effort. Yet, despite all that, my grades took a hit. I could feel the gap between where I wanted to be and where I was growing wider with each passing week. In semester two, it all caught up with me. My teachers sat me down and, with sympathetic looks, told me the hard truth: my grades weren't good. I had failed a few exams, and the sting of failure hit me hard. It felt like all the work I had put in was for nothing.

My effort, the long hours I spent studying, all seemed futile. The disappointment was overwhelming. I remember leaving that conversation feeling so, so low, like I had let everyone down—my teachers, my family, and most of all, myself. But it was that moment of hitting rock bottom that changed everything. There's something about reaching a point where you have nothing left to lose—it ignites a fire inside you. With only one month left before finals, I knew I had a choice: either I could let the weight of failure keep me down, or I could push harder than I ever had before. I chose the latter. If I was going to fail again, it wasn't going to be because I didn't try. It wasn't going to be because I held back or gave up too soon. I made a decision that no matter what, I would put in everything I had. From that moment on, I almost tripled my efforts. The days grew longer and the nights shorter, as I stayed up late into the night, pushing through exhaustion and doubt. Every minute of the day felt like it was dedicated to my studies—whether I was going over notes, solving problems, or asking questions. There were moments when I felt utterly drained, but I reminded myself that this was my chance to turn things around. I couldn't afford to waste any more time. I also started staying back after school to get help from my teachers. I had never leaned on them so much before, but I knew that I couldn't do this alone. To my surprise, they were incredibly supportive.

They saw how badly I wanted to improve, how determined I was to make up for the lost time. Little by little, I could feel the shift. The concepts that once felt so far out of reach started making sense. My confidence began to grow, not all at once, but slowly, with each small victory. The pieces were starting to fall into place. By semester three, all my teachers noticed the change. They weren't just seeing better grades on my assignments—they were seeing a different version of me, one who was more focused, more resilient, and more determined than ever before. Their praise felt good, but what mattered most was how I felt about myself. I was proud. Not just because I had improved, but because I had pushed past the failure that once seemed insurmountable and had come out stronger on the other side.

That's when I finally understood something crucial—failure wasn't the end of my journey; it was part of it. Without failing, I would never have understood the true value of hard work, the importance of perseverance, and the strength that comes from not giving up when things seem impossible. It was through that failure that I learned what I was truly capable of. It taught me that success isn't about avoiding setbacks—it's about how you rise after them. Every stumble, every low point, had brought me to this moment of growth and achievement. In the end, I realized that failure wasn't my enemy. It was my greatest teacher. It had shown me how far I could push myself, how much I could grow, and how deeply I could change. And in the process, I discovered something even more important than academic success—I discovered the strength within me to overcome any challenge, no matter how hard it seemed. It was only when I failed that I truly hit rock bottom.

In that moment, everything seemed to crumble, and I questioned whether I would ever be able to turn things around. But as low as I felt, I also realized that there was only one direction left to go—up. Rock bottom wasn't the end; it was a starting point. It was from that point of complete vulnerability and defeat that I began to climb. The climb wasn't easy. It took everything I had. Late nights, early mornings, asking for help when I would have rather stayed silent, facing my fears of inadequacy and pushing through the exhaustion. But every small victory—every extra hour of study, every concept I finally understood—was a step upward. And as I climbed, I began to gain momentum. With each small success, my confidence grew. Slowly but surely, the weight of failure started to lift, replaced by a sense of purpose and determination. Once I started climbing, it was only then that I began to realize just how far I could go. The limits I had once set for myself were fading away, and in their place was a newfound belief in my own resilience. I began to see that failure hadn't defined me—it had refined me. It had taught me lessons I could never have learned from success alone. It showed me the value of persistence, the importance of grit, and the strength that comes from getting back up after falling. Failure isn't the opposite of success; it's an essential part of it. Without failure, you don't learn. Without failure, you don't grow. And without failure, you can't fully appreciate the view from the top. When you've been at the bottom, feeling the weight of everything pushing down on you, the moment you rise above it becomes all the more meaningful.

It's in that contrast—between where you've been and where you're going—that you gain true perspective. The journey from failure to success isn't a straight line; it's a winding path with ups and downs, and that's what makes it worthwhile. When I looked back, I realized that hitting rock bottom wasn't the end of the road—it was the beginning of a new chapter, one filled with resilience, hard work, and the knowledge that success isn't about avoiding failure. It's about learning from it and using it as fuel to propel you forwar

PART IV

Do you ever wish you had a time machine? I remember being 8 years old when I hurt my leg—nothing major, just a little mishap. But to 8-year-old me, it was the end of the world. As I sat there crying in the hospital room, the doctor looked at me and said, 'Wish you had a time machine so this never could have happened, huh?' At the time, I nodded without hesitation. Of course, I wished it hadn't happened. Who wouldn't want to erase the pain in that moment? But now, as I reflect on that question 9 years later, I find myself thinking about it differently. What if I did have a time machine? Would I really go back and change that moment—or any of the others where things didn't go as planned?

As much as the idea of avoiding pain and mistakes sounds tempting, I realize that every moment, even the difficult ones, has played a part in shaping who I am today." If I had a time machine and the opportunity to go back and fix the things I once thought were mistakes, the truth is, I wouldn't change a thing. Every single experience, no matter how painful, awkward, or difficult, has shaped me into who I am today. It's tempting to imagine a life where everything went perfectly, where I didn't trip over my own two feet, or make decisions that I'd later question. But what kind of life would that be? Without the struggle, without the falls, how would I have learned to pick myself up and keep moving forward? Mistakes aren't just missteps; they're the cracks in the pavement that make you stumble, the unexpected detours that pull you off course. But those cracks don't define your path—they build it.

When you fall, it's like hitting the ground hard, feeling the sting of failure. Yet, every time you push yourself back up, you're not the same person who hit the ground. You're a little stronger, a little wiser. Each rise after a fall is like watching yourself grow taller, finding strength in places you never thought to look. Imagine the journey of self-discovery as a rugged trail—uneven, full of twists, rocks, and roots that trip you up. If I could go back and smooth out that trail, erase the obstacles, it might seem easier, but it would also be emptier. Every bruise, every stumble on that path taught me something—how to navigate the rough patches, how to pace myself, and how to keep moving forward, no matter how many times I lost my footing. Removing those moments would be like erasing the very lessons that helped me persevere. Without those scars, how would I ever know the strength that lies beneath them? Would I have wanted to experience losing that gold medal to settle for a silver? Would have wanted to bleed in my ballet shoes on stage? Should I have spent that night before a paper on my phone? Should I have cycled without a helmet, knee and shin guards? Well...no obviously. But I didn't know that. Its only when we make our mistakes, that you realize that you wouldn't change a thing, because every misstep was a step forward, a door to growth, and a path to the person I am becoming. Life's not about avoiding mistakes, it's about embracing them and learning to walk—even run—through them. In my own life, if I could go back, sure, there are moments I wish I could have avoided at the time. But in hindsight, I can see that those moments weren't there to break me—they were there to build me.

When I failed, I learned what true success feels like. When I fell down, I learned how much strength it takes to stand back up. Without these moments, I wouldn't be who I am today. We spend so much time wishing we could rewrite the past, but what we don't realize is that the past is what equips us for the future. Perfection is a myth. Life is unpredictable, messy, and sometimes chaotic, but it's in those unpredictable moments that we discover the most about ourselves. The highs are great, but the lows? They're where real growth happens. It's in the moments of failure that I learned the value of our beliefs especially in ourselves, in the moments of uncertainty that I developed clarity, and in the moments of loss that I found new strength. These experiences don't hold us back—they propel us forward, carving out who we're meant to be. If we spend our time trying to perfect every detail or erase the uncomfortable moments, we miss out on the richness that life offers. It's in the ups and downs, the wrong turns and surprises, that life truly designs itself. Like a puzzle, each piece—whether beautiful or jagged—fits together to form something far greater than we could have imagined. By embracing every aspect, every flaw, we allow our journey to unfold in the most authentic way possible, revealing a life not designed by perfection, but by experience, growth, and true fulfillment. In the end, it's not about the mistakes themselves, but what we choose to do with them. Do we let them define us, or do we use them to push ourselves further? I choose the latter. Because I know that every time I've stumbled, I've gotten back up stronger than before, and that's worth far more than any idea of perfection.

It reminds me of something Ted Mosby once said in *How I Met Your Mother*: "You can't skip ahead to where you think your life should be." Ted was always chasing the perfect outcome, always wishing he could get to the happy ending without going through the tough parts. But the tough parts, the heartaches, the mistakes—they're what shape us. Ted realized he couldn't get there without enduring the messy, imperfect moments along the way. In one of his more reflective moments, Ted said, "You can't design your life like a building." This line perfectly encapsulated his journey of growth. Like everyone else, like all of us , Ted made mistakes—plenty of them. From failed relationships to impulsive decisions, he found himself constantly tripping over his own idealism. He loved the idea of control, of shaping life into a perfect story, but through his misadventures, Ted learned that mistakes weren't setbacks; they were necessary experiences. Each misstep you take isn't just another failure, but a lesson about love, timing, and personal growth. You eventually understand that without those heartbreaks and blunders, you never would have learnt what it was like to deal with such circumstances or how to fight them. The mistakes—the wrong loves, the embarrassing moments, the awkward encounters and our cringy moments are not our undoing but rather in fact our lead to our becoming. Ted's journey shows us that it's not about avoiding mistakes, but about learning from them. He tried so hard to design his life, only to realize that life had its own design in store for him, the unforeseen obstacles, and the mistakes that gave his life depth and meaning. The story of Ted Mosby wasn't just about finding love; it was about growing through the process, about understanding that the struggles are what make the end of the journey so worthwhile. In the end, Ted realized what we all need to learn: you can't rush through life trying to avoid the bumps. You have to live it fully, embrace the mistakes, and let those moments shape you into the person you're meant to be. Without them, Ted wouldn't have learned how to appreciate the real thing when it finally came along. Your mistakes are not obstacles to overcome; they are stepping stones, guiding you to new opportunities and growth. Every wrong turn or misstep is not an ending, but rather the beginning of a new chapter in your life. They shape you into someone stronger, wiser, and more prepared for the future. Because no one learns to run before they crawl, every mistake teaches us something we couldn't have known otherwise.

The blunders, the cringe-worthy moments we wish we could erase, are not our undoing—they are our becoming. They form the foundation of who we are today, and without them, we wouldn't have the depth, resilience, and wisdom that we now possess. Mistakes force us to slow down and reflect, to gain a new perspective on the paths we're taking. Each failure teaches us how to stand taller, how to embrace challenges, and how to move forward with a deeper understanding of ourselves and the world. If we avoid mistakes, we avoid growth. But when we embrace every flaw, every uncomfortable moment, we allow ourselves to expand beyond our limitations and step into the person we're meant to be. The version of you that stands today wouldn't exist without the person who stumbled yesterday. So don't fear making mistakes—fear not learning from them. Every misstep is a door to new possibilities, and with each door you open, you walk further into the person you're destined to become. So, no time machine for me. The past is exactly as it should be: a beautiful mess that led to where I am now.

PART V

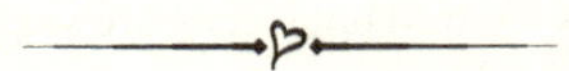

What does it mean to exist? A question that people spend most of their lives in attempts to find answers. Biology says we are to survive and reproduce. Nihilism says life has no intrinsic meaning, purpose, or value. Religions says we should spread word of god, spread love or fulfil your duties and attain peace.Cosmologically we can say life is a natural consequence of the universe's physical laws, emerging from the complex interactions of matter and energy. The meaning of life is a deeply personal and complex question with no universally accepted answer. But ultimately, each person may find their own unique sense of purpose and meaning. Yet the question is unanswered . What it mean to exist? are we our feelings? thoughts? actions? beliefs? relationships? our experiences ? To exist means to experience life as a dynamic overlap of our feelings, thoughts, actions, beliefs, relationships, and experiences. These aspects of our lives intertwine to create a sense of self that is ever-evolving. So how do we ultimately define ourselves? Maybe the answer lies in the realization that we are not meant to be defined by any single part of our being. We are more than just the sum of our emotions or the fleeting nature of our thoughts. We are not simply the things we do or the beliefs we hold, nor are we merely the relationships we cultivate or the experiences we gather. We are all of these things—woven together in an intricate, ever-changing tapestry that reflects the depth and breadth of our humanity.

Existence, in its rawest form, is a journey of becoming. Each moment, each breath, adds a new thread to this tapestry, and every one of those threads is coloured by something different—whether it's the joy we feel in connection with a loved one, the doubt that clouds our minds in moments of fear, or the quiet reflection that comes after a long day. Often we find the strings of our life unravelling into a mess and we are left with nothing but loose ends, but life gets easier when you understands these strings need to come undone so that a new story can be woven back together again. Your new life, will cost you your old one . To exist is to be caught in a constant state of becoming, a dance between the things we understand and the vast unknown. Life is not a series of destinations where we finally figure out who we are and what we're meant to be. It's more like a river, flowing and changing, winding through moments of clarity and stretches of doubt. And while we often look for concrete answers—something to hold on to, something to define us—it's the very absence of those certainties that makes our existence meaningful. The truth is, we are many things, all at once.

We are everything we have ever felt, thought, done, and believed, stitched together into a patchwork of contradictions that, when seen from afar, form the unique and beautiful pattern of who we are. And sometimes its only when we see the story woven from afar can we appreciate it. We are all of these moments, shifting and evolving in ways that we often don't realize until we look back. Defining ourselves isn't about finding one label or purpose; it's about embracing the complexity of our existence, understanding that we are a blend of contradictions, of strengths and weaknesses, of moments of clarity and times of confusion There's something profoundly freeing in this realization. To exist means we are not bound to be one thing, to feel one way, or to believe one truth.

We are allowed to be hopeful and broken, sometimes within the same breath.

We can carry strength in one hand and vulnerability in the other. We can be lost one day and found the next, and neither state is permanent. The beauty of existence is in the fact that we are never finished—we are constantly evolving, adapting, learning, and unlearning. And through this process, we grow into versions of ourselves that we could never have imagined, versions that are richer, fuller, and more complex because of the experiences we accumulate along the way. But it's not always easy to embrace this ambiguity. There are moments when the weight of not knowing feels too heavy to bear—when the uncertainty of life seems like a burden instead of a gift. In those moments, it's tempting to wish for the comfort of certainty, to long for a solid identity, a clear purpose, something to anchor us.

Yet, the magic of existence is that we don't need to have all the answers to live fully. We don't need to know exactly where we're going or who we are to make the most of the journey. The courage comes in showing up, in continuing to move forward even when the path is unclear. It's in trusting that, despite the uncertainty, there is value in every step we take, in every connection we make, in every choice we face. And maybe that's the truest form of existence—showing up, even when we're unsure, even when we're scared. It's in the way we choose to love, the way we choose to feel about it despite the risk of heartbreak. It's in the way we choose to hope, even when the world feels heavy. It's in the way we choose to be vulnerable, to open ourselves up to others, even when it would be easier to hide. To exist is to embrace the messiness of life, to find meaning not in the perfect moments, but in the imperfect ones. It's in the laughter that comes after tears, in the strength that emerges after failure, in the love that grows even after loss.

This is the essence of being human: the willingness to keep going, to keep believing in ourselves, and to keep creating meaning, even when the answers aren't clear. In the end, perhaps existence isn't something that can be neatly defined or fully understood. It's not a puzzle to be solved but a story to be lived. And that story—your story—unfolds in the way you choose to live, love, and connect, moment by moment. You are not just your feelings, thoughts, actions, or beliefs. You are the sum of all these things, constantly shifting, constantly growing. And as long as you keep showing up, keep trying, keep believing—even when the road is difficult, even when you don't have all the answers—you are living the fullest expression of existence. That, in itself, is enough. The meaning of life is not found in answers but in the way you continue to exist, to move, to love, and to become.

PART VI

As a girl living in todays world, we are expected to do amazing things from everyone. There will always be an expectation. Be it your mother and father who wants to see you grow into the best version of yourself, be it your friends who just want to see you happy, be it teachers who want to see you score marks and excel and maintain discipline or even be it the judgemental people who want you to fit into their own idea of what you should be. But what does it mean? There are even expectations from yourself, of the person who you should be, who you aspire to be, who you want to become. I think the role of expectations is one we cant escape from anywhere. The women in my life have played more than significant roles in shaping who I am today .Every woman has taught me, showed me and made me a better person. My mother, my sisters, my teachers and my friends.

I love my best friends—Viha, Devanshi, and Safanah—not just for the joy and laughter they bring into my life, but for how they've shaped me into a better version of myself. Each of them, in their own unique way, has taught me lessons I could never have learned alone. The unwavering honesty and fierce loyalty remind me of the value of authenticity in friendship. The strength and deep empathy you receive from a female friendship has taught me that true friendship is about listening, understanding, and being there when words aren't enough. Having seen each other grow up and knowing each other longer than we haven't makes you realize that friendship is not just about shared experiences, but about growth—about pushing each other to become kinder, braver, and more resilient. They are my mirrors, reflecting back the person I strive to be, and in their company, I have found the strength to chase my dreams and the courage to face my fears. Developing our characters side by side for our entire lives, I couldn't have asked for better friends.

Younger siblings often look up to their older sisters, mimicking their behaviors, learning from their actions, and seeking their approval.I take after my older sister Shanaia .Shanaia my older sister has always been a guiding light through my toughest hardships. Growing up, I often found myself in similar situations as she did, making the same mistakes she had once made. Yet instead of frustration or judgment, she offers me wisdom drawn from her own experiences. She has never failed to understand not only what went wrong but how I can learn and grow from it. The comfort in having an older sister is something that can never be replaced. She can never be replaced.I woudnt trade her for anything in the world even if I was a beggar. All the late night conversations and facetimes trying to hold our laughter and in all my strength I strive to be like my older sister.

My younger sisters Hrimaya , Neo, Sophia ,Laila and Maya , on the other hand, represents a reflection of my younger self, reminding me of a time when the world felt simple and full of possibilities. Sometimes I see myself in them. My fears, my happiness, my stupidity and my intelligence. They carry an innocence and purity that I once held, and through my eyes, I see the same curiosity and wonder I used to possess. I find myself feeling protective over them wanting to guide them as our older sister has guided me. In many ways, I feel responsible for those five , hoping they avoids the mistakes I've made while also letting them experience the world for themselves. Their wide-eyed view of life fills me with hope and reminds me how far I've come. Watching them grow at different rates is like reliving my own past all over again, and I'm filled with a mix of nostalgia and a fierce desire to shield them from the harsh realities of life, even though I know that part of growing up means facing those challenges. The teachers in my life have played more than a significant role in shaping my thinking and my perspective in the world.

A female teacher has the potential to influence her students profoundly, playing roles that can include being a role model, mentor, and nurturer. The teacher affects their academic accomplishments and molds their characters as they teach them responsibility, discipline, and care. In addition, this female teacher contributes to the special perspectives that are always welcome in the classroom by allowing every voice to be heard. They take the students through their knowledge and compassion for realizing their potential while instilling confidence, above all else, in young girls to pursue ambitions without any bindings or limitations. These teachers have encouraged me to push boundaries, break stereotypes, and take pride in their abilities. They foster an environment where young women feel safe to express themselves, take risks, and make mistakes, knowing they have someone in their corner who understands their experiences. This empowerment goes beyond academic achievement—it teaches me the importance of self-worth, emotional resilience, and the value of their voices. Remi Miss is the English teacher who first showed me what it means to push beyond my limits. Before meeting her, I never realized how much I was capable of, but she saw something in me that I didn't see in myself. She constantly challenged me to strive for more, to never settle for mediocrity, and to always aim to be the best version of myself. Shreya Miss has seen me grow in ways that few others have. She didn't just see my progress in terms of grades or performance—she saw my personal evolution. She's helped me understand that growth isn't always linear, that setbacks are part of the process, and that becoming a better person requires patience, self-reflection, and determination. Her advocation for the morally right thing to do and her ablity to stay grounded is something I aspire to learn. In moments when I doubted my abilities, her faith in me felt more profound because she knew the internal struggles I faced—ones that many women encounter, like battling self-doubt, the fear of not being enough, or the pressure to prove ourselves Manisha Miss my childhood English teacher of 5 years has seen me at my academic worst, during times when I felt like I would never succeed. She didn't just teach me the content; she taught me how to learn, how to approach challenges with a growth mindset, and how to turn failure into motivation.

Heena Miss, my counselor, has been an incredible source of support and empowerment. She has a way of making me feel seen and heard, helping me navigate the emotional and psychological hurdles that come with being a student. She's helped me understand that my worth is not tied to my grades or achievements, but to who I am as a person. Urvashi Miss her faith in my ability to improve has been a constant source of motivation, and I've always felt that she genuinely cared about my journey, not just as a student but as a human being.

And to make me reflect even deeper I look to a younger girl at my school, a junior, who reminds me so much of myself when I was her age. Watching her go through the same phases of uncertainty and growth fills me with a sense of responsibility. I want to be there for her, to guide her as others have guided me, and to help her navigate the challenges that come with being a student. At the same time, I admire her youthful energy and the excitement with which she approaches life.

And one to the woman who started it all, my mother. She has been my constant source of guidance, teaching me the importance of empathy, patience, and perseverance. In her, I see the definition of true courage—not the loud, heroic kind, but the quiet endurance that carries on even when no one is watching. My mother's ability to balance her own dreams while nurturing mine has shown me what it means to care for others without losing sight of yourself. She has taught me that vulnerability is not a weakness but a strength, and that kindness is a power often underestimated. Her sacrifices have inspired me to strive for more, not out of obligation, but out of gratitude for all she has given. In her journey, I see the possibilities for my own, and through her example, I've learned to stand tall, be compassionate, and believe in my potential. She's the reason I aspire to be better, not just for myself, but for the people I love. To all the women like my mother, sisters, aunts, friends, my friends mothers and my teachers.

To be a daughter, a sister, a student, a niece and a friend is all a blessing.

I thank you all for making me the woman I am today.

PART VII

I stood at the ledge of the course overseeing the stable, in front of me, a tall, chestnut horse grazed lazily, his tail swishing away the occasional fly. He was beautiful—majestic, even. But all I could think about was the last time I had been on a horse. I must've been nine or ten years old. I remember the wind in my hair, the thrill of being up so high, the world moving beneath me. And then, in an instant, everything changed. The horse I had been riding spooked, his powerful body jolting sideways. I lost control, felt myself slipping, and before I knew it, I was on the ground. My breath knocked out of me, my body aching, and tears streaming down my face. The confusion, the mud staining my clothes and I could feel the warmth of my blood drip down my knees , the sharp edge of the rick I fell on, the trainers footsteps increasing as he rushed to me. The fall had been hard—painful, yes—but it wasn't the physical hurt that had stayed with me.

It was the fear. Since that day, I never got back on a horse. I watched from a distance as friends and family rode, smiling and laughing, but I couldn't bring myself to join them. It was as if every time I thought about riding again, I was that little girl on the ground, afraid, embarrassed, and hurt. I let that one moment define me. The fear had grown so deep that I convinced myself that maybe I wasn't meant to ride. But today was different. Something had changed. I had spent too many years letting that fear rule me, holding me back from something I once loved. It wasn't just about the horse anymore—it was about me. I was tired of living with the weight of that fear. So, here I was, standing at the edge of the corral, heart pounding, but determined. I got up and out of the car and walked towards the arena.I felt the cold wind settle on my face and I was greeted by the familiar smell of corn that came from the vendors roasting them nearby. I took a deep breath and stepped forward, my boots crunching in the wet gravel beneath me. My hands trembled slightly as I approached the horse. Ahead of me stood Rusty, his chestnut coat gleaming in the late afternoon sun, muscles rippling beneath his sleek skin as he shifted his weight. He was massive—towering over me, a gentle giant in every sense—but the sight of him made my heart race, the familiar fear tightening its grip around my chest. As I got closer, the scent of hay and leather filled my nose, grounding me for just a second. My fingers, still shaky, hovered in the air before finally brushing against his warm, velvety coat. His skin twitched under my touch, but Rusty remained calm, his large, dark eyes meeting mine with a kind of quiet understanding.

I hesitated, feeling that familiar knot of dread tightening in my stomach. *What if I fall again? What if I can't do it?* The doubts swirled around me like a storm, but I closed my eyes and reminded myself of why I was here. I wasn't that scared little girl anymore. I wasn't defined by that one moment. I had changed, grown, and I wasn't going to let my past hold me prisoner.

Slowly, I grabbed the reins and led Rusty to the mounting block. My heart was pounding so hard I thought it might burst out of my chest, but I focused on my breathing, one step at a time. My foot found the stirrup, and with a shaky exhale, I lifted myself into the saddle. I sat there for a moment, gripping the reins, feeling Rusty shift beneath me. The ground felt so far away, and for a split second, I was that little girl again, who fell from a horse 8 years ago in this very same course.

For a split second I could feel myself falling and I could see the ground right before hitting it. But , was that who I am? Am I still that person? Who is held back by fear? No, how could I be? I knew that while our past experiences shape us, they do not have to define us indefinitely. I gave a gentle nudge with my heels, and Rusty began to walk. The world seemed to move in slow motion at first, my body stiff and tense, every muscle ready for something to go wrong. But as we made our way around the arena, something unexpected happened. I began to relax. The rhythmic movement of Rusty's steps, the sway of his body beneath me—it was soothing. Familiar, even. I took a deep breath and allowed myself to look around, really look. The sun was setting, casting a golden glow over the landscape, the fog in the distant mountains reflected the suns warmth contrasting their usual grey colours The wind rustled through the trees, and for the first time in a long time, I felt...free.

The fear was still there, lurking in the background, but it didn't control me. Not anymore. We made another lap around the corral, and I felt a smile tug at the corners of my lips. The fear was still there, yes, but it was fading with every step, replaced by something I hadn't felt in years—confidence. I had done it. I was riding again. As we came to a stop, I slid down from the saddle, my legs shaky but strong. I patted Rusty's neck, a flood of emotions swirling inside me. Relief, pride, joy—but most of all, freedom. I had spent so long believing that my fall defined me, that it would always be a part of who I was. But standing there, I realized something important: I wasn't that scared little girl anymore. The fall was a part of my story, but it wasn't the end of it. I looked at Rusty, standing calmly by my side, and smiled. It wasn't just about riding a horse today. It was about reclaiming a part of myself that I had lost. It was about proving to myself that while I was a product of my past, I didn't have to be a prisoner to it. I could move forward, grow, and maybe even fly again. And as I walked back toward the stable, I knew that I had taken the first step toward something new, something better. The past was behind me, but it didn't define me. I was free. I've come to realize a powerful truth: we are all products of our past, but we don't have to remain prisoners to them.

This concept hit home for me when I faced my fear of riding horses Every experience I've had, whether joyous or painful, has contributed to the tapestry of my identity. The fear of falling, the embarrassment of that moment long ago, and the hesitation that kept me from pursuing something I loved—all of these elements are part of my narrative. They have shaped the lens through which I view the world and myself. However, I now understand that while these experiences influence me, they do not have to dictate my future. In choosing to confront my fear of riding again, I realized that I could redefine my relationship with my past. Instead of allowing that single moment of trauma to cast a long shadow over my life, I could acknowledge it as just one chapter among many. I learned that growth comes not from avoiding challenges but from facing them head-on, from transforming fear into strength and vulnerability into resilience.

This shift in perspective has empowered me to take control of my life. I am learning to embrace new opportunities, even those that make my heart race with apprehension. Each time I step out of my comfort zone, whether by trying something new or revisiting a past fear, I am reclaiming a part of myself. I am rewriting my story, infusing it with hope, courage, and possibility. I've come to recognize that I have the power to choose how I respond to life's challenges. I can allow fear to paralyze me or let it fuel my determination to grow. I can see each setback as an opportunity to learn and evolve rather than a reason to retreat. With each new experience, I gather more tools for my journey, building a toolkit of resilience, confidence, and self-acceptance. With each passing day I've learned that my story is mine to write. While I cannot change the past, I can choose how I respond to it and how it influences my journey moving forward. I can choose to embrace the lessons it offers while refusing to let it define my worth or potential.

PART VIII

The piano's melody crept through the air like a haunting lullaby, each note pulling me deeper into the void of the studio, where time lost all meaning. The music wasn't soothing anymore—it felt sinister, its soft tones a cruel contrast to the agony building inside me. My feet were trapped in the unforgiving embrace of my pointe shoes, the skin beneath rubbed raw, each step a flash of searing pain. But it wasn't just my feet. The ache crawled up my legs, twisting into every muscle, digging into my bones, threatening to consume me whole. I stared at the mirror, but my reflection was foreign—taut, brittle and I was about to shatter. My breath was shallow, each inhale a fight to push down the dread tightening in my chest. My eyes darted toward the instructor, knowing her gaze would land on me at any second. The fear prickled down my spine before I even heard her voice. Back straight, arms higher!" Her command lashed out which made my body flinch but it was out of fear I obeyed automatically, but inside, I was crumbling. Sweat dripped down my temple, but it felt like ice, freezing on my skin. My shoulders screamed in protest as I forced them into submission, the muscles quivering beneath the unbearable pressure.

The pain wasn't just physical anymore—it was something deeper, something that gnawed at my mind, hollowing me out from the inside. My shoulder were on fire and it fire like every muscle was being pulled and pushed into its breaking point. My vision blurred as I blinked back tears that threatened to spill, but I swallowed them down, burying them deep. Tears were weakness. Weakness was failure. And failure was unforgivable. My mind raced, filled with the ticking of a clock I couldn't see but felt pounding in my skull. The time stretched on forever, the seconds bleeding into each other, the pain festering, spreading like a disease. My body was burning, yet freezing, every nerve alight with sensation, but dulled by the numbness that began to creep in. I wanted to scream, to rip off the shoes, to let the pain explode out of me in one final release, but I couldn't. Instead, I forced a breath, shallow, trembling, barely enough to keep me standing. The voice in my head, darker, crueler than the instructor's, whispered: *You're not good enough. You'll never be good enough. Why even try?* It wasn't the instructor I feared—it was that voice, the one I couldn't escape no matter how hard I pushed. The one that lingered long after the music stopped. And yet, despite the darkness clawing at me, despite the agony pulsing through every inch of my body, I held my pose. Because I had no choice.

Anything less than perfection would mean letting the fear win. And in this moment, the pain was the only thing I had control over. The only thing that made me feel alive. I had learned early on that in ballet, there was no room for weakness. No place to hide from the mistakes that haunted me after every class. And so I held my pose, even as my body screamed for relief, even as my spirit sagged beneath the weight of dread. Because in ballet, anything less than perfection wasn't just inadequate—it was unthinkable. Ballet, notorious for its physical demands. Your pointe shoes create blisters, your muscles ache from endless practice, and the body is pushed to its limits, a dancer sees the pain as temporary, a necessary sacrifice on the path to excellence. Days blurred into weeks, each class an endless cycle of the same movements, the same pain, the same harsh commands.

It was a drill—one I couldn't escape. I would arrive at the studio knowing what awaited me: the familiar sting of muscles pushed past their limits, the burning in my lungs as I tried to keep up with the relentless pace. But no matter how much I prepared, nothing dulled the fear that gripped me every time I stepped into the room. The perfection demanded wasn't a goal, it was a requirement. And I felt its weight press down on me like a boulder, crushing any semblance of ease or joy. Each plié, each arabesque, felt like a battle. And I was fighting—not just against my body, but against the part of me that wanted to stop. I had been taught that there were no shortcuts in ballet. No room for mediocrity. Every pirouette, every leap had to be flawless. The tiniest mistake was met with sharp criticism, and even when I thought I had done well, there was always something more to correct.

My reflection in the mirror was never quite good enough. The physical pain was one thing. My feet bled in those pointe shoes; the bones in my ankles felt like they might snap, and my back ached with a dull, persistent throb and I felt sharp shooting pains in my calves. But the mental strain was far worse. It was a suffocating pressure that sat on my chest, growing heavier with each passing day. In ballet, there was no room for excuses. It didn't matter if you were tired, if your muscles were torn, or if your mind was fraying at the edges. You showed up. You danced. And you gave everything, even when you had nothing left to give. It was suffering and sacrifice, but it was also survival. I had learned to find a twisted comfort in the agony. The blisters on my feet were badges of honor. The ache in my legs was proof that I was pushing myself. And the relentless pursuit of perfection was the only thing that kept me going. Ballet had become more than just a dance. It was a way of life. It had seeped into every corner of my mind, rewiring how I thought about myself and the world.

Pain was temporary. Weakness was unacceptable. Perfection was everything. And so I danced. Even when my body cried out for mercy, even when my spirit felt like it was breaking, I danced. Because ballet had taught me one unshakable truth: to succeed, you had to endure. To rise above, you had to embrace the pain and use it as fuel. And I was determined to rise. For every bruise, every scar, every hour spent locked in that studio, there was something greater waiting on the other side—something worth all the suffering. Ballet had given me discipline, and with that discipline came strength. In the end, the pain wasn't my enemy. It was my teacher. But that's when I realised , I can only let my pain define me and wear me away if I let it.

I was meant to use it, to become better, to become greater, to become the best. All the bruises and cuts and aches , they weren't signs of weakness or pain but in fact a symbolism of grit and hard work . Grit is defined as grit is a positive, non-cognitive trait based on a person's perseverance of effort combined with their passion for a particular long-term goal or end state. This perseverance of effort helps people overcome obstacles or challenges to accomplishment and drives people to achieve. And that's what I had. Grit. I learned that there will be days where it feels like the whole world is against you and its only in that moment where still show up regardless of the pain and how it destroys you. Ballet taught and hit me several times and made me fall into failure but it also shaped me into a person who got back up. Its not about how many times you get hit or how hard you fall, its how you choose it get back up .

PART IX

The tent was filled with gasps of awe as the acrobat swung through the air, a vision of grace and daring. The woman in the audience clutched the edge of her seat, her eyes wide, heart racing not just from the thrill of the performance but from the ache of **what could have been**. As a child, she had dreamed of becoming an acrobat. She spent hours imagining herself flying through the air, defying gravity, her body in perfect harmony with the ropes and the sky. But life had pulled her in other directions. School, family expectations, and practicality had all nudged her off that path. Now, sitting in the audience, she felt a deep pang of regret. The acrobat moved with a freedom she longed for, and she couldn't stop wondering what her life would have been like if she had pursued her dream. Could that have been her up there, dancing with the air? Would she have felt that rush of adrenaline, that soaring joy? Instead, she had chosen a different life, one filled with responsibilities and routines that had weighed her down. And now, watching someone else live the dream she had let slip away, she felt the sharp sting of loss. The regret of not chasing her childhood dream filled her chest, heavy and unshakable. As the acrobat took her final bow, the audience applauded, and the woman clapped too, her hands moving automatically. But inside, all she could think of was the version of herself that could have been up there – the fearless child who had once believed she could fly.

But, why? Why do we limit ourselves and not push ourselves to our true limit and settle for less? The fear of failure looms large, casting a shadow over our aspirations. This anxiety often freezes them us place, making the thought of taking risks feel overwhelming. The prospect of falling short of their our own expectations—or those of others—can lead to inaction and a relentless cycle of self-doubt. As we retreat from challenges, opportunities slip away, leaving them trapped in a loop of hesitation. We also trap ourselves in comfort zones which provide a reassuring sense of familiarity, a safe haven where the routine feels secure. Yet, this safety comes at a cost: the dreams left unpursued. Stepping outside this bubble requires a brave heart, one willing to face the discomfort that accompanies growth. Unfortunately, many find the idea of confronting that unease more intimidating than the prospect of settling for less.

Yes, within this turmoil, self-doubt emerges as a powerful barrier, an insidious force that stifles ambition and desire. When people lack confidence in their abilities or worthiness, every step toward their aspirations can feel monumental. In the shadows of our aspirations, self-doubt emerges as a formidable barrier, an insidious force that coils around our hearts and stifles the very ambition that fuels our dreams. Each whisper of insecurity creeps in, entwining itself with our thoughts, suffocating our hopes with a relentless grip. In these moments, our confidence evaporates, and every stride toward our goals feels monumental, laden with the weight of invisible chains. We find ourselves ensnared in a suffocating cycle of negative self-talk, a relentless echo of lies that reverberates in the chambers of our minds. Each day becomes a battle, a silent war against the internal critic that insists we are not enough. It's a cage of our own making, fashioned from the shards of our fears and perceptions, trapping us in a prison of our own design. But fear, fear is the biggest and the worst tool that can be used against you.

Your fear is a liability, your limitation. It convinces us to sell ourselves short, to shrink into the shadows, and to believe that we are unworthy of our own dreams. It wraps itself around our hearts, tightens its grip, and blurs the contours of our aspirations. What we fail to grasp in our darkest hours is that this fear is not an innate part of us; it is a narrative woven by society, a web of expectations and doubts spun to keep us from soaring beyond the constraints of our own existence. We sit, paralyzed, in this self-imposed cage, clutching the key of potential, but too afraid to turn it, to unlock the doors to our true selves. Fear often masquerades as a wise counsel, whispering softly in our ears, "You can't do it," or "You're not good enough." Yet, beneath its veneer of protective wisdom lies a deceptive truth. Fear is a liar, a treacherous companion that leads us astray from the paths of our potential. It convinces us that our dreams are unattainable, painting a bleak picture of the consequences of our aspirations. This distortion of reality keeps us from seeing the possibilities that exist beyond our comfort zones.

We fail to recognize that fear is a cage crafted from our own insecurities and doubts. With each negative thought we entertain, we add another bar to this prison, fortifying our confinement. As we sit within these self-imposed walls, we become paralyzed, our hearts heavy with the weight of imagined failures. We may cling to our fears as if they were shields, believing that they keep us safe from the risks of the world. Yet, what we fail to realize is that we are the architects of our own captivity. The key to our liberation rests in our hands, yet we hesitate to turn it, paralyzed by the very fears we have created. The narrative of fear is not innate; it is a story told to us by a society that often values conformity over creativity, security over exploration. From an early age, we absorb the messages that instill fear—warnings of failure, tales of regret, and the pressure to adhere to traditional paths. These narratives shape our understanding of what it means to pursue our passions, embedding in us the belief that stepping outside our comfort zones is a perilous endeavor. In doing so, fear becomes a societal construct, designed to keep us tethered to the ground while the stars of our dreams twinkle just out of reach. In truth, the very essence of fear is rooted in the unknown. It thrives on uncertainty, feeding on our anxiety about the future. When we confront the unknown, fear often raises its voice, drowning out our inner desires with a cacophony of "What ifs?" and "I can'ts." But it is crucial to understand that the unknown is not an enemy; it is a canvas waiting for us to paint our dreams upon. Just as a child learns to ride a bicycle by facing the uncertainty of balance, so too can we navigate our fears by embracing the possibility of growth. To dismantle the cage of fear, we must first acknowledge its existence. We must confront the lies that fear tells us, exposing them to the light of reality. Every time we challenge a fear—be it the fear of failure, rejection, or inadequacy—we chip away at the bars that confine us. With each act of courage, we begin to realize that the only limits that truly exist are those we impose on ourselves.

You create you. You become what you think. Yet, in this swirling maelstrom of fear and doubt, we often postpone our joy, allowing our darkest fears to dictate the choices we make. How many moments of potential happiness have we sacrificed at the altar of insecurity? It is vital to recognize that fear is a liar, a deceitful specter that preys on our vulnerabilities. Not every closed door is truly locked; sometimes, all it takes is the courage to lean against it, to push gently and see what lies beyond. So, why not embrace the simplicity of existence? Why not draw stick figures, transforming the mundane into the whimsical? Why not sing off-key, letting your voice soar without the weight of judgment? Write bad poems. Flirt clumsily, allowing vulnerability to blossom in the awkwardness. Play video games on easy mode, releasing the chains of expectation. The truth is, you do not need to be exceptional to find joy in the act itself. Embrace the beautifully messy, imperfect journey that is your life. Let go of the relentless desire to climb every tree flawlessly; instead, climb for the sheer thrill of the experience, for the way the wind brushes against your skin, and the way the world looks from above, regardless of the outcome. Each act can birth joy, foster connections, and sow seeds of fulfillment—far more valuable than the unattainable pursuit of perfection. In the end, it is about reclaiming your narrative, rewriting the script that has long been dictated by fear and doubt. It is about pushing against the boundaries that confine you, about daring to dance with uncertainty, and allowing yourself to revel in the exquisite freedom of exploration. When you liberate yourself from the shackles of self-doubt and fear, you unlock the door to a life where joy flourishes in abundance, where creativity flows freely like a river unrestrained, and where every step you take, no matter how clumsy or uncertain, becomes a heartfelt celebration of the intricate, beautiful journey that is uniquely yours. In this journey of becoming, let each moment resonate within you, a reminder that to be alive is to embrace the full spectrum of experience—the heartaches, the triumphs, the missteps, and the joys. And in this embrace, may you find not just yourself but also the courage to chase the wild, wonderful dreams that have always lived within you, waiting patiently for the moment you choose to set them free.

PART X

6th October 2024, that when I realized. I realized who I was. It took everything in me to embrace who I was and finally nothing in me to push my true self away. The morning was chaotic. My mind was torn between my upcoming math test and the excitement of the Garba celebration later that evening. The school was buzzing with preparations for the event, but I had barely noticed, lost in my sea of formulas and equations. Then, in the middle of my spiral, my phone buzzed. It was my friend texting me "Hey, can you help me with something? I need an outfit for Garba, and I have no idea what to wear!" "Sure, I'll help you,' I said She came over, and we dove headfirst into the mess of fabric and color, flipping through skirts and dupattas like our lives depended on it. We discussed matching sets, colour coordinating our own outfits, what will look good in photos, but then somewhere five minutes in we weren't really talking about clothes. We were talking about life—the real stuff, the things that make your heart race and your stomach twist. We laughed at the ridiculousness of it all, how everything feels like it's about to explode when you're trying to juggle school, friends, family, and expectations. Somewhere in the middle of that mess, I realized something about myself. I was a good friend. It sounds small, almost trivial, but it wasn't. I cared. I showed up. I made time, even when it felt like I had none to give. I never gave myself enough credit for being a good friend. That realisation automatically made me smile and feel like I was worth something not just to someone else this time but myself too. Being a good friend meant I was being present, and that was powerful. I remembered times when I had needed support, the moments when I felt lost and alone. I recalled the friends who had shown up for me, their laughter pulling me out of my dark thoughts, their understanding reminding me I wasn't alone. Now, I was on the other side of that equation, and it felt amazing. Each time I offered my thoughts or encouragement, I felt a little piece of myself coming back to life. It was liberating to realize that friendship wasn't just about the fun times, the laughter, and the shared moments. It was about the weight of trust, the comfort of knowing that someone would be there for you, no matter the circumstances. As I helped my friend sift through outfits, I saw how important it was for her to feel confident and beautiful. In helping her, I wasn't just being a friend; I was affirming her worth, her individuality. and in that act of kindness, I was reminded of my own worth. I realized that being there for someone else didn't mean sacrificing my own needs; instead, it added a richness to my life. It felt good to listen to her dreams and insecurities, to empathize with her struggles, and to celebrate her successes. In a way, I was learning how to be kinder to myself. I was showing myself that I could give love and support to others, and in doing so, I was learning to love myself a little more. For too long, I had been caught in a cycle of self-doubt, questioning my value and feeling like I was never enough. But in that moment, as we shared laughter and a few tears, I understood that being a good friend meant being vulnerable, too. It meant opening up, allowing someone else to see my true self, and trusting them with my heart. That was something worth celebrating. It felt like reclaiming a part of myself that I had buried beneath layers of insecurity and expectation.

As my friend left that day, the weight of the world felt lighter. I carried a sense of fulfillment within me—a reminder that we're all connected, that our lives are woven together by moments of kindness, laughter, and support. I had embraced my role as a friend, and it made me feel whole, reminding me that I was capable of love and compassion, not just for others, but for myself as well. In those simple moments of connection, I rediscovered a piece of who I truly was, and it felt good. It felt like home.

When she left, the house went quiet. Too quiet. The kind of silence that feels heavy.I saw the time .Three thirty, time for snacks.I went to the kitchen in silence, the lights still off and only the sunlight entering the hall.I sat down to eat, my plate staring back at me, cold and uninviting. No one reminded me to eat. No one checked in. It was just me, alone in this new independence that I had spent years craving. And yet, sitting there, I felt the weight of it in a way I hadn't expected. It was strange—liberating and terrifying all at once. I was finally free to make my own choices, to move through the world without anyone telling me what to do. But with that freedom came the realization that I was no longer the person I used to be. I was grown now, making my own decisions, carving out my own space in the world. It was such a little thing, deciding to eat on my own, but it felt like the world had shifted under my feet. I realised that im hardworking . At seventeen, I found myself straddling a line between childhood and adulthood, and this realization felt like a rite of passage. I was still surrounded by family and friends, their voices and laughter filling the space around me, yet I felt an exhilarating sense of autonomy. The fact that I could choose what to put on my plate, what music to listen to while studying, or even how late I wanted to stay up was thrilling. It was as if I had stepped onto a stage, and the spotlight was finally on me. I had grown accustomed to relying on my parents for guidance, their voices echoing in my head with every decision I faced. Yet, that evening as I sat at the table alone, I felt a spark of courage that I hadn't tapped into before. I realized that all those years of support, love, and lessons had prepared me for this very moment. It wasn't that I was entirely on my own; rather, I was learning to embrace my independence while still being anchored by the foundation they had built for me. I could feel the seeds of confidence sprouting within me. They had been nurtured through years of experiences, both big and small. Each challenge I faced—whether it was a difficult math test, a tough conversation with a friend, or just navigating the highs and lows of school life—had chipped away at my insecurities, layer by layer. Every time I made a choice and saw it through, I became a little more assured, a little more self-reliant. I was discovering that adulthood wasn't solely defined by age but rather by the choices I made and the responsibilities I took on. This realization felt empowering. I had the ability to shape my day, my life, and even my future. I didn't need to seek permission or validation; I had the confidence to trust my instincts. In that moment of quiet reflection, I understood that I could carve out my own path, and that felt like a beautiful promise. The freedom I felt was intoxicating, a heady mix of possibility and excitement. I knew I could set goals for myself, whether it was studying for my exams or making plans with friends, and I could choose how to achieve them. It was exhilarating to think about the adventures that awaited me, the decisions I would make without hesitation, and the person I was becoming in the process. In embracing this independence, I realized I could navigate life's complexities with grace. I could lean on my friends for support while still standing firm in my convictions. I could ask for help when I needed it, recognizing that independence didn't mean isolation. It meant being strong enough to seek out connections while remaining true to myself. This newfound confidence was a beacon, guiding me as I stepped boldly into the future, ready to embrace whatever came my way.

I gave my test and returned home to get ready for the dance. I sat down in front of the mirror, makeup strewn across the table. I had always imagined myself transforming for a night like this, turning into someone else, someone more glamorous, more put together. So I layered it on—eyeliner, bold lipstick, glitter eyeshadow, blush that made my cheeks glow like they were lit from within. When I finally looked up, I saw someone beautiful staring back at me. Someone perfect. But perfect is a funny thing. It's seductive, like a cigarette you light even though you know it's killing you with every inhale. I was addicted to the idea of perfection, addicted to the way it made me feel powerful, in control and like the person I created was a better version of myself. But as I stared into the mirror, the girl looking back wasn't me. She was someone I had created, a polished illusion of who I thought I needed to be. And then it hit me—this wasn't me. The makeup, the image, the act—it was all a lie. A beautifully constructed lie, but a lie nonetheless. In that moment, something inside me snapped, like a rubber band stretched too far. I wiped it all away. The bright colors, the heavy makeup—it was gone in seconds, leaving me bare, raw. I felt exposed, vulnerable, but for the first time in a long time, I felt real. I don't have to fit into anyone else's expectations, I thought. I don't have to be perfect. For so long, I had sought validation from others, measuring my worth against their opinions. I believed that if I looked a certain way, acted a certain way, I would be more lovable, more interesting. But that night, as I stood in front of the mirror, I realized that I was robbing myself of the most important relationship I could have—the one with myself. It struck me that if I couldn't accept and love the person staring back at me, how could I expect anyone else to? Being true to myself meant stripping away the layers of expectation and revealing the core of my being, the part that had been buried beneath a facade of perfection. I wanted to embrace my imperfections, my quirks, my authenticity. It was essential to me that I became someone I could genuinely admire—not because of how I looked or how I fit into someone else's idea of beauty, but because of who I was inside. In that moment of vulnerability, I realized that true confidence comes from self-acceptance. I didn't need to conform to a narrow definition of beauty that was dictated by others. Instead, I could define beauty on my own terms. It was okay to have flaws, to have days when I felt less than perfect, and to allow myself to be a work in progress. This journey towards self-acceptance was not just about shedding makeup or altering my appearance; it was about shedding the need for approval. It was about understanding that my worth wasn't tied to others' perceptions of me, but rather to how I viewed myself. I wanted to be seen not just for my outward appearance but for my thoughts, my passions, my struggles, and my victories. Embracing my true self meant giving myself permission to be real and imperfect. I wanted to celebrate who I was, with all my complexities and contradictions. I realized that when I looked in the mirror, I wanted to see a person who was proud of her journey, not just her appearance. I wanted to honour my culture, my heritage, and my individuality, not as something to hide, but as something to wear boldly. And in that acceptance, I found freedom. I understood that my journey toward self-love was just beginning, but I was ready to embrace it wholeheartedly. I didn't have to pretend anymore; I could simply be me. The road ahead might be challenging, but as I stepped away from the mirror, I felt a sense of lightness, as if the weight of other people's expectations had lifted, allowing me to finally breathe.

The time of arrived, the night I had been waiting year round for garba night. The air was thick with the energy of tradition, of celebration. The music pounded through the night, pulling me in, drowning out the noise in my head. My friends surrounded me, pulling me into the circle, their laughter and joy infectious. They taught me the steps, moving to the beat, spinning under the stars. I stumbled at first, awkward and unsure, but they didn't care. They caught me, held me, kept me moving until I forgot I was ever afraid. And that's when it happened—the final, overwhelming realization. For years, I had kept a part of myself hidden away, too scared to embrace my own culture, too scared to be seen as something I didn't think I was. But standing there, in the middle of the dance, with the music swirling around me and the laughter echoing in my ears, I felt something shift inside me. This was my culture. This was my heritage. And I didn't need to hide from it anymore. I didn't need to suppress the parts of myself that I thought didn't fit into the mold I had created. I realized, with a clarity that shook me to my core, that I loved this part of myself. I loved my culture, my traditions, my history. And I loved the fact that it was mine. This was my heritage. And I didn't need to hide from it anymore. I didn't need to suppress the parts of myself that I thought didn't fit into the mold I had created. I realized, with a clarity that shook me to my core, that I loved this part of myself. I loved my culture, my traditions, my history. And I loved the fact that it was mine. Finally feeling happy in my culture was like breathing for the first time after being underwater for too long. The colors, the sounds, the rhythms—they were all pieces of a puzzle that had long been scattered, but now they came together to form a beautiful, intricate picture. In that moment, I understood the power of belonging. It wasn't just about the vibrant outfits or the electrifying dances; it was about a deep-rooted connection to something larger than myself—a community that welcomed me with open arms, a history that whispered stories of resilience and joy. Yet, it was bittersweet. I realized the value of my culture only when I had less than a year left of staying here in India. The impending move to university loomed over me like a cloud, bringing with it a fear of losing a significant part of my identity. I was terrified that once I stepped beyond the borders of my hometown, I might drift away from the very things that shaped me—my family, my language, the festivals that filled my calendar, and the shared laughter of friends around food. The thought of leaving felt like a weight on my chest, a painful tug of war between excitement for new beginnings and sadness for what I might leave behind. I had spent so long trying to fit into a box, suppressing my cultural identity in hopes of blending in with a more global narrative. Now, as the clock ticked down to my departure, I felt an urgency to embrace every part of my heritage, to hold it close and make it a vibrant tapestry of who I was. In that moment at the Garba celebration, dancing with my friends, I understood that my culture was not just something I would leave behind; it was something I could carry with me. It would not fade into the background as I ventured into new experiences. Instead, it would travel with me, embedded in my laughter, in my values, and in the stories I would share with new friends. I felt a newfound responsibility to nurture it, to honor it in every space I entered, whether in the heart of Gujarat or the bustling streets of a new city.I could see it clearly now—my culture was my anchor, the roots that would keep me grounded no matter how far I wandered. It reminded me of who I was, and as I danced that night, I could feel the pride swelling within me. I was ready to claim my identity, to shout it from the rooftops.

I am Indian, and I am proud. This realization was not just a moment; it was a promise to myself—to cherish my heritage, to live authentically, and to embrace every piece of who I was, both now and in the future. And as the music crescended around me, I knew that this celebration was more than just a dance; it was the beginning of a beautiful journey of self-acceptance. I was no longer afraid of what others might think. Instead, I was filled with a joy that came from knowing my roots would always be a part of me, no matter where life took me. The night was a blur after that. The dancing, the music, the colours—they all melted together into one perfect moment of clarity. I wasn't just someone trying to fit in. I wasn't just a girl who had to be perfect, who had to meet everyone else's expectations. I was me. And that was enough. The evening of Garba was more than just a celebration; it was a transformative moment in my life. It brought forth profound realizations about who I truly am and what I value.

The chaotic morning, the laughter shared with my friend, and the vulnerable moments spent in front of the mirror all led me to embrace my true self. I discovered that being a good friend was a reflection of my own worth, and through helping others, I found the beauty in my individuality. Sitting at the table alone, I realized that my independence was built on a foundation of resilience and effort. I had tackled the challenges of school, the weight of expectations, and the fears of stepping into adulthood. Every time I studied late into the night or pushed through a tough assignment, I was proving to myself that I could achieve my goals. I had not merely survived my journey; I had worked hard to thrive, and that realization empowered me. The freedom I felt during Garba night was an echo of the hard work I had put into preparing for that moment, both academically and personally. I had learned to embrace my culture and my identity, but I also understood that this journey was the product of my dedication and perseverance.

I was no longer just someone trying to fit in; I was a hardworking individual who had crafted her path, learned from her experiences, and discovered her worth. And as I danced beneath the stars, surrounded by the vibrant spirit of my culture, I felt a surge of pride. I realized that my heritage is not something to be concealed; it is a vital part of my identity that deserves to be celebrated. The freedom I felt in expressing my authentic self, free from the shackles of perfection, illuminated the path ahead. I understood that true confidence lies not in conforming to external expectations but in accepting and loving myself as I am. In that whirlwind of dance and joy, as I spun under the stars, I felt a profound sense of pride—not only in my cultural heritage but also in the person I had become through my efforts. I was hard-working, compassionate, and fiercely authentic. And embracing all these parts of myself felt like the ultimate victory. This journey of self-discovery has shown me the importance of connection, both with others and with myself. It has taught me that embracing vulnerability leads to deeper relationships and a more fulfilling life. Now, as I move forward, I carry these realizations with me as guiding principles: to be present, to be kind, to celebrate my uniqueness, and to embrace the beautiful tapestry of my identity. In this dance of life, I am learning to move with grace, authenticity, and joy, knowing that I am worthy, just as I am. 6th October 2024. That's when I realized. I realized who I was. It took everything in me to embrace it, to finally accept the person I had been hiding from for so long. But when I did, when I let go of the fear, the doubt, the need to be perfect, it was like a weight had been lifted. I didn't have to push my true self away anymore. She was here to stay. 6th October 2024, that's when I realized who I was. And for the first time, it felt like enough.

In Making This Book

As we reach the end, and upon one last reflection, I can't help but think—what were we here for? What is different about us? I mean, we're all the same people, aren't we? We experience the same emotions: love, anger, sadness, joy. Each of us carries our own stories, woven from threads of laughter and tears, hopes and fears. We grapple with the same questions, seeking connection in a world that can sometimes feel overwhelmingly vast. Yet, in this shared humanity lies the beauty of our existence; we are all just humans trying to love and grow. Love... just simply love. Look at all the things it brings—the quiet moments that linger, the laughter that fills empty rooms, the lightness that touches even the heaviest days. To love is to live with your heart wide open, to let the world in, and to give a part of yourself without asking for anything in return. There's a rawness in it, a beautiful kind of risk that makes you vulnerable but also makes you real. To live is to be vulnerable, and to be vulnerable is to be true—to let yourself be seen in all your messy, unguarded beauty. It feels like the whole world is happening to you, pressing in from all sides, yet you're happening to the world too—two quiet pulses meeting , creating a rhythm only you can hear.

And as you navigate this dance, don't be afraid to make mistakes; let hope linger, even if it trembles at the edges. Love is there even when it's raw, even when it aches. Be kind for no reason—kindness needs no excuse, and sometimes it's the strongest thing you have. Look up to yourself with gentle eyes—you've made it this far, walking roads that didn't wait for you to catch your breath. Learn the truth, but let it soften you rather than harden you. Don't be a stranger; love people deeply, even if it's just for a fleeting moment. Hold close the ones who feel like home, and find the quiet comfort of belonging wherever you go. Take happiness gently in your hands; don't chase it—invite it. Live like you've already won, because every day you choose to keep going is a small victory. You're here, a heartbeat in the vast universe, and yet you are the universe too—contained, breathing, alive.

And I want to end this story with a lyric from a harry styles song
"Lights up and they know who you are
Know who you are
Do you know who you are?"

This invites us to fully embrace our identities, to step into the glow and let the warmth of recognition envelop us. When the lights come on, there's a haunting beauty in being seen—both by ourselves and by those around us. It gently nudges us to ponder self-awareness, guiding us toward a deeper understanding of our purpose and our place in this sprawling, imperfect world. In this intimate journey of discovery, we find that our true essence shines brightest when we allow ourselves to be vulnerable, revealing our raw selves in all their unfiltered beauty. This openness is not just a gift to ourselves; it's a precious offering to everyone we encounter. When we learn to love ourselves, we cultivate the strength to extend that love outward—creating a ripple effect that can illuminate even the darkest corners of life.

So, as you step into your own light, now hold this truth close: you are never alone.

Now when you learn that you realise its impossible to stop, nothing can stop you. Your greatest weapon are your thoughts vut that can be used against ourselves too. A realisation of thought is a realisation to power in our identity. And in truly knowing who you are, you open the door to a life brimming with possibility, inviting joy, authenticity, and genuine relationships. Let your light shine, let your heart overflow with love, and continue to explore the boundless beauty of your existence. Remember that every moment of vulnerability is a testament to your courage, and each act of kindness sends ripples of hope into the world.

And to writing this book I have my parents to thank for their unwavering support, patience, and endless love have been my greatest strength—I have you to thank for for teaching me resilience, for always believing in me, and for encouraging me to pursue my dreams, even when the path wasn't clear. To my sisters, Hrimaya, Neo, and Shanu, who fill my life with light, laughter, and inspiration. You remind me daily of the beauty of family and the power of sisterhood. To my friends, Viha, Devanshi, and Safanah, for the laughter, understanding, and encouragement that make every challenge lighter and every success sweeter. And finally, to myself—for having the courage to start, to keep going, and to be vulnerable enough to share this journey. This book is for all of you.